The Politics of Projectile Corpses

By

Garrett James Dillon

Avantpop Publishing
2025

National Suicide Prevention Hotline
nimh.nih.gov/health/topics/suicide-prevention
Call 988

Harm Reduction Resources
harmreduction.org/resource-center/harm-
reduction-near-you

Fireside Psychedelic Peer Support Line
firesideproject.org/psychedelic-peer-support-line
623-473-7433

First Paperback Edition

ISBN 9798992685459
Poetry

Cover Art by Seth Singer

avantpopbooks.com

For Heather,
Thanks for adding positive adjectives to my vocabulary and joy filled years to my life. I never thought that I needed either; thanks for showing me that I deserved both.

"It is impossible to understand addiction without asking what relief the addict finds, or hopes to find, in the drug or the addictive behavior."

-Dr. Gabor Mate

"Give strong drink unto him that is ready to perish, and wine unto those that be heavy of hearts. Let him drink, and forget his poverty, and remember his misery no more"

-Proverbs 31:6-7

"Man will never be free until the last king is strangled with the entrails of the last priest."

-Denis Diderot

"You wish the world was clean but I'm in love with the way it's dirty."

-Johnny Hobo and the Freight Trains
"Not My Revolution"

The Politics of Projectile Corpses

Garrett James Dillon

Speedfreak

Well, at least the skeletons I'm hallucinating are smiling
As they lurk shimmering geometric between the shadows on the
wall
I crack my clenched jaw into a grin fit for a graveyard
Bid them good morning and continue on with my toxic ritual
Filling my bunker temple with a cursed fog stillborn from a filth-
pearl white glass vessel
A strong stench like diesel fumes crossed with snorted
pharmaceuticals makes itself at home
Cultivating negative energy because it's the only fuel that seems to
work for me
Powers me to pace lost and manic, looking for nowhere and
finding it everywhere
Sleep deprivation and starvation diet disorientation guide me along
this circular path
Like a broken compass under a starless night

V.W.B.O.W.

Electric twitch calls to them
Bells and lights screeching out
A siren song of false hope
Desecrated math adds up to a habit
As it sweats away from the sun

Musculature tuned to desperation
While frantic response rhythms
Ring out like gunshots on a battlefield
And leave as many victors behind

Untitled

Bled dry and begging for the sunrise
I wring out my sleeves for leftover tricks
hoping for some counterfeit salvation
or at the very least a loose Seroquel
but find nothing except battery acid and bullet casings,
glass eyeballs and loaded dice,
wasted wreckage like relics to be
hoarded and worshiped by headless mannequins frozen
in obscene poses as they wait for their chance to scream

The enemy of my enemy is my only friend now
as the butterflies embrace cannibalism
and the shadows dance in agony down unnamed roads
littered with crosses and confetti towards treasures too
terrible for our pitiful language to describe

The madmen who once raved about armageddon in the streets
have all gone mute, and speak to us now by way of a
dead, unblinking stare the color of diseased milk
stretching 99 miles in every direction

It is the only joke left to laugh at
and the only gospel left to suffer for

It is the only promise that cannot be broken
And the only truth that will ever set you free

A Suicide Funeral In Texas

My father was one of the first officers to respond to the scene
"Deceased male, 30s, self inflicted gunshot wound to the head"
My father tells me David left a note.

He has never shared the contents with anyone as far as I know.
I can say with certainty he's never shared them with me

I returned to Texas for the funeral, the same reason I was there
last time
I felt like a withered wreath: only appearing in cemeteries amongst
grief
Never joyous rice flung at weddings
Or celebratory cigars at births
Just a crow on a tombstone
Resting until he's ready to fly away to something shiny

"Suicide" is a word that is whispered in small town Texas
People employ euphemisms and speak in hushed tones
The weight of Christian shame crushes all conversations about
mental health
Replacing it instead with some stripe of Protestant pastor's pathetic
excuse for a eulogy
Assuring us halfheartedly with jerry-rigged scripture that all sins
are forgivable
Including the one his Church will say straightforward any other
Sunday is not
The one whose name he couldn't even work up the balls, decency
or honor to speak

4

He was a coward in a collar promising divine reunification to a
crowd that needed to believe it
Even if it inconveniently contradicted everything the church had
taught them to accept
About the fiery final resting place of every other victim of the
exact same fate
whose names and faces the crowd did not know well enough to
resort to heresy as a salve
I sat gritting my teeth godless, fists
clenched but face calm as sorrow boiled into hatred

When the afterlife is discussed during the ride to Arlington
National Cemetery for the burial
They asked me, the lone atheist in the front car carrying the closest
family members in the funeral procession, the question :

"Where do you think David is now?"

I declined to answer politely and looked out the window instead
Doing my damnedest to dissociate as they talked about how he's
hugging his father in heaven
Because my honest answer was "he's in the back of the hearse one
car ahead of us with half of his fucking skull missing"
And that is not what anyone wanted to hear
So while they comforted each other clinging to their holy hopes
I mourned silently in my disbelief as we entered the graveyards gate
Because even if heaven is real and that's where he is
I will never see my Uncle David again

So after serving as a pallbearer
And feeling the weight of his corpse release from my grip as we
fed him to the manicured earth

After the 21 gun salute and the final words of mourning and remembrance from loved ones
I watched the coffin descend, completing his permanent transition from a person to a memory
A fresh scar that never heals and itches and bleeds both randomly and on cue
On days like today, the 7 year anniversary of the night he left us all behind
Or the day I got his name tattooed under the Metallica logo on my right bicep, just like he had
Or when I saw them live and stood with my hat off for the entirety of "Fade to Black"
Or for that matter any time I let that song play all the way through, always in solitude so I can cry freely
I grieve deeply in a way I can't talk about to anyone else on that side of the family

Because as they all kneeled together and said "until we meet again"
I had to stand there all alone as the the only one who said "good bye"

"Dustin's Huffing Dustoff"

"This here is a clown family goddamnit, and we'll burn that way together!"

Dustin screamed at an empty apartment
Devoid of all other life save for black mold and silverfish
Flicking a box-cutter in and out as he paced amongst old newspapers
Stacked to the ceiling or scattered on the floor
Chain-smoking cheap cigarettes covered in burns and scars
He checks the peephole every minute and a half in vain
The smell of carcinogens would overwhelm even the most unreal of company
The taste of poison is his only companion under constantly flickering lights
And the sound of the dripping faucet serves as a metronome to his mundane madness
Numbness is the only gift he's ever received
And he clutches it's aluminum vessel like a golden handgun
Depleted muscles twitch in his wrist as he
Puts the business end in his mouth and pulls the trigger
The Do Not Resuscitate bracelet dances on desperate sweat
Steady til the seizure kicks in, the only thing he's ever earned
Then the inevitable collapse as all 3 take a final bow
The mold and the bugs will eat better tonight Than Dustin had in months or even years
And the final tragedy in a long line of fantastic tragedies
Is the waste of a can only half empty
Gripped in a rigor mortis fist

Roadkill Sally

Hot coffee and a blunt for breakfast
Roadkill Sally rides at dawn
As asphalt fries up blood like eggs
And the radio blasts out her favorite song

She is the queen of the maggots
Impure priestess of rotted flesh
Scanning the streets for skulls and bones
Sweet is the smell of death so fresh

Spotting a specimen she licks her lips
And flicks her roach as she pulls to the side
Roadkill Sally will take things from here
Living life only to collect what has died

Lion's Food

Oh, to be godless in a godly place
Blessed against our will by minority rule mandate
And anointed in gunpowder on a weekly basis
Yesterday grips a garrote behind you
The men of god flash their teeth in a grin
And wait with a saint's patience to hear the gnashing of yours

Here in the land of coat-hangers and confession booths
Of broken promises and crumbled walls
Where men in robes speak for god but hear only cash registers
Trying their damnedest to trade sodomy for segregation at the
courthouse
Their sacred salvation cooked down to a campaign slogan
To be dispatched as gospel in trademark pogrom cadence

There are no heretics amongst them
No deviance from some lost righteousness to re-thread the
narrative
No better angels to grovel to under this blinding light, no

God's America is functioning exactly as it was intended to
        The snake handlers have quit gambling and embraced the
        Gadsden shuffle
        Those who speak in tongues whisper to power in a more
        univer$al language
        The Calvinists preach predestination with a cheat sheet in
        their wallet
        The priests lick their lips as they count fresh meat orphans
        like rosary beads in the dark

9

These are truly the men of Jehovah
> The god who drowned his children as they clawed at the Ark
> Whose chosen people he let be enslaved then paid for their
> freedom with innocent blood
> Who raped a child so his only son could be tortured to death
> for his own failures
> Who blessed us with diseased life and then cursed us to be
> cured of it

"And every knee
Shall bow"

Ichthyoallyeinotoxism

There are plenty of fish in the sea
But most won't get you high
And many are the wrong kind of toxic
Their flesh nutritious at best
Most are good for simple survival And not much else

The depths are vast and crushing
Filled with predators getting fat
And prey without a prayer
Sitting in silt I look towards the stars
The sand behind me is warm
I'm not going fishing tonight

In Your Ruins

Your life is an abandoned building
Rotting and decaying
Feeble foundation betraying
Your worthless walls and empty filling

The lights are on, but no one is home
It's got broken windows
And creaks when the wind blows
It might as well be glass, but I'll throw no stones

I'm no longer a resident of that cursed tenement
So why commission
A demolition
When its collapse is surely imminent?

And in your ruins I'll dance evermore
To rejoice in your rubble
Will have been worth all the trouble
That started the day I first opened your door

Stimulant

Goddamn this
Endless Tachycardia Ritual
Toothless and blind
In the piss yellow moonlight

I was screaming invocations
For Minor demons
And more rum
Scarification like starlight
Peering out underneath it all

Witches Teeth

I get by on spells and potions
A wizard born too late and breaking down too early
My hands shake as I caress the syringe like a sigil
Filled with the sticky black earth magick
Of Luddlowe's nightmares and Baudelaire's dreams
Descended from Occult tradition and lacquered upon a 2mg emerald
Alchemy reborn in the pharmaceutical age
I nod into the blissful abyss ritual
Head bowed down in narcotic meditation
Eschewing enlightenment for dark medication
See, the Law of Equivalent Exchange can't be broken like a cheap pill
You can't gain anything in this life without losing something of
equal or greater value
So I'll feast on Witches Teeth til I slip into amnesiac slumber
And wake up zombified to mysterious and infected bite marks

One day you are what you eat
And then you wake up to find
That you are what you are eaten by

Eulogy For A Local Sexpot

Now you fucked up
The whore deer ovulates at gunpoint
Dinosaurs set all the clocks to 4:20
Business is business plain and simple
Whether it's staplers or popcorn
Dreamcatchers or PCP

Self involved to the point of psychosis
Everyone is Forest Whitaker now
The glory hole calls again
It rapes your churches and burns your women
But this is still the best acid trip ever
Pour out some mouthwash on the concrete
Pour some Kool-Aid in the ocean

You have fucked up now
The whore killed his parents with a full bladder
St. Peter has had enough
Satan lives in a volcano
God wants you to wear a hat

Prescribed suicide just to end up in Pet Heaven
Your pony is dead and dogs love boobs
And Daddy loves donkeys
It's super crazy sexy
It's not opposite day
IT'S SATURDAY
Happy Birthday Rick

Let's Party

5002 S. Maryland Parkway

The present is fucked and I have no use for it
So I'm blacking out today in reverence of days past
Pernicious but precious, yesteryear is preferable
Back when the suffering at least made sense

Just a drugged up druid hunkered down in his bunker temple
Leaving trash strewn about to honor the forgotten
Forgetting the dead to placate the living
Choosing not to choose life as if life were an option
Opting instead for dread and infestation
With all the grace of a fist through a mirror

I stepped on more broken glass inside than outside
Just ask the bloody footprints leading to the liquor store

    Past the madmen screaming in the street
    Burnt a shade of copper that can't be ripped from their skin

    Past the college students avoiding eye contact
    Waiting for their buses and their futures far away from here

    Past the dive bars and punk clubs and crack houses
    Resolute in their toxic charm and reliable cheap escapes

Sanguine staggered pattern tells a stripped down story
It's particulars are all irrelevant, ignoble, illegal

The neighborhood was nice and negative
It was the kind of place salvation came hard
Filth as a way of life was my spirituality then

Nourished daily by ritualistic roach sacrifices
The spilt yeast eucharist ensured a healthy harvest
Every day I'd giveth and every night I'd taketh away

When I sank home into my holiest of holes
There was always something for me to kill

$108.35

Fresh air is fine but I've had better
Inhaling deep the breath of dissociative angels
Those imperfect messengers and unreliable narrators
Who speak in riddles that tickle my spine and drain my wallet
Then sing a distorted chorus as I exit their inverted paradise
Returning wild eyed and neutralized to a place some might call home
But the angels, they call to me and so back down I go
All spirituality is transactional, I just like to keep the receipt
To fold it up into an origami albatross and set it on fire
Watching the flames suck in the oxygen greedily
Before burning up and blowing away down dirty streets
I watch and feel nothing but a strange kinship and intense cravings
In my experience that's better than feeling nothing at all

Kiara

She died in December
And was buried in January
But once upon a time she smiled in the summertime
Freckled and mischievous
And we frolicked in the fall
Downing bongloads and shoplifting malt liquor
Hopping fences and swimming on shrooms in the moonlight
She'd feed me kpins when I was having a bad trip
And I was her getaway driver on drunken nights
When she'd ditch her grandparents house on a day pass from
Seven Hills Behavioral Hospital
We kissed once on ecstasy
   The second time we met
     But don't give me the third degree,
       we kept it pushing platonic
         And moved forth as fast friends

I fell in love with a woman and cut ties with female homies to
alleviate her paranoia
A projection, I would later learn, of the guilt she felt for her own
infidelity
And so I wasn't there when the pills got too expensive and
something cheaper crept in like a cancer
Or when the flame from her lighter moved from tinfoil to a spoon
I thought nothing of long sleeves in the fall once we reconnected
Slurred speech was an integral aspect of our shared language
And so the secret stared straight at me with pinpoint pupils and I
still didn't see it
I wasn't there until I was, but by then it was too late
I threw a rose on her casket before she was buried

19

Six months later I shoved pills in the same dirt as I sobbed
uncontrollably
Breaking up a fat bud and rubbing it into the grass as my blood
approximated pure vodka
I tried to beg a devil that doesn't exist for a deal that he wouldn't
have agreed to anyway
I found a way to hate a god that doesn't exist even more than I
already did
But the raw reality I have to live with is that I lost one of the best
friends I've ever had the privilege of knowing
And the undying guilt and regret of having discarded like debris
Because I thought there was always tomorrow to make things right
again
And I had no one to blame but myself when tomorrow came for me
But left her behind for yesterday to to keep frozen in finality

She was here until she wasn't
Don't wait for tomorrow
It's always on time, so you better not be late

Sunday Morning Not Coming Down

My, my, my
My mutilated mycelium
Washed down with cheap grains finest offerings
With one nostril painted white as a coroner's sheet
And the other stinging with the smell of sea salt void key
The balloons have long been deflated
The liquor flows like sacrificial blood
It is Sunday morning and brother I am not coming down
Instead I preside as priest over this boiling marriage of cocaine and
baking soda
Put the blackened spoon on ice to consecrate
And watch embryonic ghosts form from the foam
Sniffles and switchblades as they and my arteries harden
Followed by the deepest breaths possible as I bring them together

#19

When writhing through the void
Molotov eyeballs pointed north to Reno
Or dimmed forward bidding hostile hellos
Receiving gifts of barbed wire and Robitussin
From strangers walking by
And remaining strangers after they pass

You might want to start investing in downers
After you kick your doors down and your mirrors in
After life destroys you but death does not want you
After staring down the duel barrels
of yesterday and tomorrow
For a thousand todays
Hands done shaking but still thirsty against homeostasis
This noose tied and untied again and again

Soon
You will understand
Something in yourself will be killed
Sooner than you'd like to think
And it will fester and be fed upon
Just like the rest of us

Trigger

Writing this poem is a trigger

The tyranny of the blank page spits in my face
The seconds tick past at a sedative pace
No lines on the mirror, no lines on the screen
My bag of tricks has been dumped out, ripped open and licked clean

The words come out wrong if they come out at all
Not enough inspiration and too much alcohol
Not sure if I'm a poet lacking his muse in painful longing
Or a coke fiend with too much free time and a laptop not worth
pawning

I've got a feeling it's time for a new fuel
One that doesn't leave me strung out as the sun rises so cruel
Courting psychosis cornered and crashed out
Checking my bank account but there ain't no funds to cash out

So I spend my last two bucks on a 32 of high life
Stroll on indifferent to death because that's the story of my life
And I scream at the coffee drinkers as they drive to get their
morning fix
"You goddamn caffeine addicts need to grow up, you fuckin
yuppies you make me sick!"

Fiending

Man I've spent a lot of time tripping
But this time I've fallen hard
And I don't wanna get up

Makes my heart flutter like methamphetamine
Gets rid of my worries like a handful of Xanax
Now I'm in holes so often it's like I'm hooked on ketamine
Never used a needle but it's stuck in my blood and well, that tracks

More euphoric than a Dutch ecstasy pill
More addictive than pure Colombian coke
I can't wrap my head around this strange new thrill
Gets me higher than anything I've popped, snorted or smoked

And that's no short list my friends, if you didn't know rest assured
From Acid to Zolpidem, sweet Satan I've had myself a time
Lost plenty of cash to the traphouse but never been robbed of my
words

This is one of the trickiest poems I've written, it's not about
misery, fuck it even rhymes!

Now don't get me wrong because I'm not getting right
I'm still eating the alphabet and washing it down with booze
But none of those things can help my withdrawals tonight
I'm hungry for the only fix that'll get me right, darlin I'm fiending
for you

Mortals On The 22nd Floor

The angels on the 23rd floor
Tap frenzied songs on frosty mirrors
In their sunless heaven
Giggling and gagging on smoke and flesh
We dance to their music because it's free
And we never sleep at the witching hour anyway

The demons on 2
Are smashing their internal clocks in the lobby
In their mania they pick up the pieces of glass
Blessing them as scalpels before inscribing their flesh
With answerless riddles and disturbing jokes
We don't understand the language
But laugh hysterically all the same
I guess you just had to be there to get it

Those bastard skeletons on 13 owe us money
Never lend money to creatures without pockets
Or pants
Or skin
They sneak into our closets so they can hide in plain sight
Smiling empty in every way possible

But it's the ghosts across the hall that worry me the most
They look far too familiar in a way we can't figure out
And know our names but won't tell us theirs
No matter how hard we pound bloodied knuckles
On the only door without a number
Or how long we scream threats and apologies and gibberish

In a hallway with no mirrors or clocks
No apparitions poke out to validate our venom

Because we are just mortals on the 22nd floor
Drowning our sorrows out on the balcony
And trying our best not to look down

Going Downhill

I'm going downhill
And I've never felt better
The wind in my face
Sober hearts do race
Trying to find my place

I'm going downhill
But my future's looking up
Chemicals do flow
Chemicals I know
Sweet release, just let go

I'm going downhill
But I'm making progress up
Saturday sober
At least 'til day is over
Staff sergeant turned frontline soldier

I'm going downhill
But she keeps my spirits up
Satanic priestess
She leaves me speechless
Riding hard down the steepness

I'm going downhill
And I've never felt better
And if I eat shit
It won't hurt a bit
Just give me a kiss and give me a hit

Icebox Canyon

Amongst dead ferns and living oaks
I feel serenity in my insignificance
Beneath the ancient mountains
Where ice melts and brings peace instead of madness
The sound of a flowing stream negates the static screeching
Of a dead city frequency I am now blissfully out of range of
My lover inspects the waters for tadpoles
As I meditate on erosion patterns

The flying insects hover above my cannabis
I burn one down as I look up
Clouds billow into their brethren above
And I enjoy the higher elevation below

Blacked Out Blues

Waking up once more
To an empty bottle in a lonely bed
With my head throbbing with regrets trickling in like the first rains
of a flood
As the fragmented memories form incomplete and horrific
Like a smug sneer with a few front teeth knocked out

I blink my sandpaper eyelids open so I can take stock of what's left
in the sadistic sunlight

My phone is lost so I can't call and ask for a forgiveness I don't
deserve
For transgressions I cannot recall whatsoever outside of worn out
unlucky guesses

My keys were confiscated to stop me from driving when I couldn't
even stand up
To finish a fight I can't remember the cause of
With a person whose face I ever knew

Most concerning to me is my missing bottle of pills
No doubt hidden from me so I couldn't add a few downers for desert
A caustic combination I swear by as the antidote to both sickness
and health
Which commonly causes me to break out in
Mysterious bruises and all too familiar scars

I've never met the man I was that night, the same man I've been
many nights and days before
But I've heard enough to know for a fact he is my mortal enemy

A malevolent spirit that dwells in my shadow, watches and waits
for my steps to stagger
And when my senses leave my body he steps in and does his finest art

My woman didn't stay the night and I don't blame her
She gets anxious being alone with even the most stable of strangers
So when she spoke the word "unsafe" it cut through the blank
darkness like a dagger
Missed that other bastard and pierced my temporarily sobered heart
And so here I suffer in solitude and ponder my possession, unable
to exorcise
It will inevitably come down to me or him and my indecision is
wearing thin
Because this game is getting old, or so I am told by the heretics
and the faithful
And so are me and my downfall bent doppelganger
Or so I am told by those who don't have to kill part of themselves
to stay alive

Return of the Flightless Balloons

Taking flight amongst balloons that will never be inflated to rise
Gutter destiny slumped cornered where it is welcome
A quiet place to ponder the adhesive properties of a spiders web
Or the politics of far-off poppy fields guarded by U.S. troops
With heads bowed forward in servile gratitude for a ripped off relief
As cigarettes burn through dirt on indifferent fingers

Familiar faces sink and scab over into different familiar faces
Faces long gone, skin decayed a distinct shade of gray that started
as pale blue in the lips
Faces on headstones with fading smiles nourished by tributes of
tequila and tears

The phantom miasma of vinegar and burnt foil creeps in once more
Hangs in the air like a weighted noose swinging slowly back and forth
A perennial haunting that returns after every exorcism
A curse right on cue; wretched like clockwork counting desperate
seconds
A thief in the night that robs us of that which we hold dearest
Sometimes we catch it in the act and cast it out with empty pockets
But it simply strolls away immortal knowing our address
And so once again we close the door but don't lock it

Life Goes Fast (Take It Slow)

I've been awake for three long days off that
Methamphetamine and lemon haze again
What can I say, I'm just stuck in my ways my friend

Still not tired though I've walked so far
For a fist full of Ambien and xannie bars

'Cuz I think I need to get some sleep, maybe
In my bed or maybe 6 feet deep, baby
And I don't get there by counting sheep, ya see

Still my dreams are no place for peace
Nothing but nightmares which never cease

So I

Picked up a bottle to drown my sorrows
But they're always there when I awake tomorrow

I guess joy's not owned, it's only borrowed

One day soon we will pay what we owe
Life goes fast so just take it slow
Yeah, life goes fast so just take it slow

Ketamine Moon

Turned on with the safety off
My nightmares come true and gnaw my bones
Dancing with a hospital gown
Or drowning in moonlight
You know exactly what you are
Been this way since fractured memory can recall
Necromancers funeral so full of dull surprises

They found me baptized in vodka
Biting rats in consecrated darkness
And I found them boring and predictable
Lost valor seizing up underneath comatose stars

I lost them under a hornet sun
Subsisting on sand and other crystalline landscapes
Guided by futility through my cursed quest to understand
This thirst that begs for relief with no exceptions
This hunger that knows no defeat or death

Home Is Where The Bar Never Closes

Home is where the bars never close
And the Christians have no political power
A Nuclear neon valley nestled beneath a burnt out sky
We murdered the North Star and are now guided by the STRAT
Towards an abundance of sublime beauties both natural and synthetic
In this overstimulated oasis where the desert water dances in
defiance of god

So I put some Silver Haze into the skeletal wind and hope it carries
it to the sagebrush beyond
Drunk on open alcohol and warm winter's sun, I wander the cities
sleepless streets
I have snorted fish-scale cocaine in top floor hotel suites above
I have smoked shake n bake meth in the lawless wash tunnels below
Might have been pick-pocketed by a slot machine or two for the
greater good
But I'll take those odds over the taxman's any 24 hour day of the year

The house may always win but at least I live in the neighborhood

The truth is that this illicit parasite illusion paradise
Is the only place I've ever lived where I could be myself, for better
or worse
I had no say in my birth but
GODDAMNIT
          I will be buried, scattered or dissolved in Las Vegas, Nevada
               Home sweet home until hell takes me

Weirdness In Austin

Here in the land of broth drinkers and hell raisers
Where red lights are just suggestions to the new 1%
And the illegal smell of unholy smoke
That canonized Willie as a state hero patron saint
Wafts free within the oppressive and humid air
A city south by southwest
In a county with no limits
Where the stars at night
Are big and bright
Deep in the only part of Texas that has a heart
We marvel at the architecture of the skyscrapers from the creek
And the architecture of the bars from the floor

Ex green book properties
Turned ex punk bars
Now stillborn again as a gentrified graveyard where the mediocre
go to bury the legends
The writing on the tombstones spell out the great plundering
underway that's just getting started

So while capitalist Cali transplants scan Dirty 6 with bleach eyes
We'll just be snorting coke in the back of a hearse parked illegally
outside a jazz show
Feeling just fine with being the filth that their cash couldn't kill to
cleanse

Inner Depths///Outer Lands

Oxygen deprivation ceremonial dance
Summons stars in my ceiling underneath the atrophied night sky
Binge linguistics send communiques through collapsed portals
Flesh twitches off kilter kinetic; currently the current flows
backwards
The Ethos of a High Voltage Discipline

The Sacred Arts of Distortion and Distraction
Taught without breath or effort from Inner depths
Outer lands wait eagerly for your imperfect caress
A freelance agent for the Department of Chaos
No prayers or apologies memorized
Free as goods stolen from a thief

Where The Wicked Are Welcome

I can't fucking stand the smell of burning sage
My roommates will occasionally "cleanse" the house in this way
Smokeshop bargain *brujeria* intended to fend off bad vibes and evil
spirits
The irony is lost on no one, but my rent is paid in full so I'm not
going anywhere
I just shut my door and smoke dope until they're done, and then I
smoke some more
The thick marijuana clouds forming a safe haven for demons that I
don't even believe in

My ex-girlfriend who lives upstairs complains of sleep paralysis
I respond with pieces of Xanax like cut up bandages

My other friend warns me of the dangers of "negative vibrations"
I steal his magic mushrooms and try to find the frequency

And yet,

There are no monsters underneath my bed
    My curses are all self-inflicted and well documented at this point
        And the only things that keep me up at night were
            bought for that exact purpose

I'm the only resident to not yet suffer some sort of foot wound
And the only resident that walks barefoot on beer runs to the
corner store
Dancing through the broken glass minefields of Smoke Ranch
sidewalks

And returning unscarred, always

My money is on materialism, that these are just coincidences in a
world of chaos
And that nothing lit up inside the house matters as long as it
doesn't burn the fucker down
But sometimes I get a kick by looking at it from the sageburners
point of view
I gave shelter to wicked forces in their time of need and now they
return the favor

Who knows?
Maybe it's good to have imaginary friends in very low places

Garrett James Dillon has control over everything yet controls nothing at all. He's a fever dream prospering in a surreal reality, releasing words like a shotgun blast to the reader's chest. No other writer since Charles Bukowski and William S. Burroughs has captured the hallucinatory essence of darkness concurrently weaving in the luminescent glow of pure bliss seen whilst looking up from the gutter. The Politics of Projectile Corpses is a book of poetry for the hedonistic punk anarchist who lives in us all. @garrett.james.dillon